In 1935 if you wanted to
read a good book, you needed
either a lot of money or a library card.
Cheap paperbacks were available, but their
poor production generally mirrored the quality
between the covers. One weekend that year,
Allen Lane, Managing Director of The Bodley Head,
having spent the weekend visiting Agatha Christie,
found himself on a platform at Exeter station trying to
find something to read for his journey back to London.
He was appalled by the quality of the material he had to
choose from. Everything that Allen Lane achieved from that
day until his death in 1970 was based on a passionate belief
in the existence of 'a vast reading public for *intelligent*
books at a low price'. The result of his momentous vision
was the birth not only of Penguin, but of the 'paperback
revolution'. Quality writing became available for the price of
a packet of cigarettes, literature became a mass medium
for the first time, a nation of book-borrowers became a
nation of book-buyers – and the very concept of book
publishing was changed for ever. Those founding
principles – of quality and value, with an overarching
belief in the fundamental importance of reading –
have guided everything the company has
done since 1935. Sir Allen Lane's
pioneering spirit is still very much alive
at Penguin in 2005. Here's to
the next 70 years!

MORE THAN A BUSINESS

'We decided it was time to end the almost customary half-hearted manner in which cheap editions were produced – as though the only people who could possibly want cheap editions must belong to a lower order of intelligence. We, however, believed in the existence in this country of a vast reading public for intelligent books at a low price, and staked everything on it'
Sir Allen Lane, 1902–1970

'The Penguin Books are splendid value for sixpence, so splendid that if other publishers had any sense they would combine against them and suppress them'
George Orwell

'More than a business … a national cultural asset'
Guardian

'When you look at the whole Penguin achievement you know that it constitutes, in action, one of the more democratic successes of our recent social history'
Richard Hoggart

Letters from Four Seasons

ALISTAIR COOKE

PENGUIN BOOKS

PENGUIN BOOKS

Published by the Penguin Group
Penguin Books Ltd, 80 Strand, London WC2R ORL, England
Penguin Group (USA) Inc., 375 Hudson Street, New York, New York 10014, USA
Penguin Group (Canada), 10 Alcorn Avenue, Toronto, Ontario, Canada M4V 3B2
(a division of Pearson Penguin Canada Inc.)
Penguin Ireland, 25 St Stephen's Green, Dublin 2, Ireland
(a division of Penguin Books Ltd)
Penguin Group (Australia), 250 Camberwell Road, Camberwell, Victoria 3124,
Australia (a division of Pearson Australia Group Pty Ltd)
Penguin Books India Pvt Ltd, 11 Community Centre,
Panchsheel Park, New Delhi – 110 017, India
Penguin Group (NZ), cnr Airborne and Rosedale Roads, Albany,
Auckland 1310, New Zealand (a division of Pearson New Zealand Ltd)
Penguin Books (South Africa) (Pty) Ltd, 24 Sturdee Avenue,
Rosebank 2196, South Africa

Penguin Books Ltd, Registered Offices: 80 Strand, London WC2R ORL, England

www.penguin.com

Letter from America: 1946–2004 first published
by Allen Lane 2004
These extracts and additional letters published
as a Pocket Penguin 2005

1

Set in 11/13pt Monotype Dante
Typeset by Palimpsest Book Production Limited
Polmont, Stirlingshire
Printed in England by Clays Ltd, St Ives plc

Contents

Spring

Summer

Fall

Winter

Spring

Memories of Augusta

11 April 1997

My oldest friend, by now in both senses, deeply resents putting the clock forward in the spring because, as he puts it, 'it spoils the evening news'. By which he means that at 6.30 every evening, the main news time, he likes to draw the curtains on a darkening sky. But, after last Sunday's time change, 6.30 is still daylight, and this old curmudgeon doesn't want to watch the world's troubles by daylight. So he draws the heavy curtains just the same, blots out every chink of light, grumbles, pours his favourite painkiller and settles down. Being close to his vintage, I often drop down the avenue to watch the news with him. I'd likely do this if I was a mere acquaintance, for, as somebody said, 'After the age of eighty, all contemporaries are friends.'

Well, the other night, we were sitting there, five small lamps on in his study, and the telly, everything, suddenly went *bam*, to black. He had to totter to the door to let in a shaft of light. It seems that someone, it would have to have been his wife, had put on in the kitchen a toaster and the microwave while the dishwasher was throbbing away. It was too much, so: a blown fuse. The old man's wife is the mechanic in his household, and pretty soon she'd thrown the switch, and Thomas Edison's invention blazed into life again. The old man's comment was: 'What sort of a civilization is this, anyway?'

An ironical comment indeed. The first image that came flashing in on the screen was of immense flooding, people in lumber jackets staggering into each other to amass sandbags against the rising river, and doing it during a blizzard. It was up in Minnesota and the Dakotas, the people, over a stretch of land about half the size of Ireland, being visited by a weird combination: a late winter blizzard and the early upsurge of the usual spring floods. And here he was, complaining of the momentary failure of one link in the elaborate chain of electronic comfort we live by.

Well, I'm sorry. I'd meant to begin on a cheerful note, for I look out of my study window now and suddenly – after a wild succession of wind and sun and bitter cold and then 70-degree days, I look out, and suddenly the fuzz of Central Park's woods has turned to sprightly green blossom. And around a bend of the reservoir the forsythia is out and the white dogwood and that tree about which an English poet, by a simple switch of words, produced a memorable line: 'Loveliest of trees, the cherry now'.

So, I'm sure, I hope, lots of people feel as I do: that whatever horrors are recorded on the evening news –

in Bosnia, in Zaire, in Jerusalem, wherever – our guilt is a little softened by the arrival of the marvellous spring. A terrific Anglophile I know once said, at this time of year, 'Oh, to be in England, now that spring is there'. My wife said, 'Oh, to be anywhere now that spring is there'. Correct.

And this weekend in particular, I think of one place more than another that I might be, where I have been going for just over thirty years, but go no more. Down to Augusta, Georgia – the only place on earth I believe where the best in the world play golf in a sumptuous botanical garden: three hundred and sixty-five rolling acres with their towering Georgia pines, and the azalea bushes, and the white dogwood, and the pink dogwood, and the magnolias and firethorn and redbud and yellow jasmine – all the native flowers of Georgia and beyond. Not planted in plots – nothing remotely as disciplined and sergeant-majored as a French garden. Rather, bushes and spreads along the creeks and meadows, here and there and everywhere. Not by accident. By a thunderbolt of God's grace or nature's – however you prefer to say it. This is how this vast garden came about.

For nobody knows how long, this tract of land in Georgia had been an indigo farm. Indigo was, after cotton, the South's most profitable export. But in the early 1850s a Belgian baron and his son, both horticulturalists, newly arrived in America, liked the look of this rolling land in a valley, and were taken by the plantation house, only just built, a low, colonial-style, arcaded, white house, flanked by two wings of slave quarters. The baron bought the place in 1857, and began to convert it into what was to become the South's first commercial nursery. He and his son searched the Southland for particular flowers. They imported trees and plants from around the world. Within three years they issued a catalogue listing thirteen hundred varieties of pear and nine hundred varieties of apple. They were set to be early millionaires when there sounded the guns of Fort Sumter – the opening of the Civil War (1860–65, if it helps). The plantation was turned for the duration into a fruit farm for the provision of the Confederate armies. After the war, there's no record that their fruit farm, called Fruitlands, was a howling success. Trees and flowers (more than saleable fruits) were their passion. Well, the father died, and in 1910, the son died and left the property to his widow and his two sons. The story is blurred at this point, but evidently they didn't see eye to eye about running a nursery. They divided the property, sold it, and moved away from Augusta. The land remained partly fruit farm, partly large open meadows until the middle 1920s, when there arrived in Augusta a very mid-1920s type, so stereotyped he went into the musical comedies of Richard Rodgers and Kern and Gershwin, a real-estate tycoon with two-toned shoes and a roving eye: one Commodore Stoltz. It was the time of the Florida land boom when long stretches of beach (of ocean, you might almost say) were filled in, and hotels built on them. Sometimes the excited investors up north learned that the hotels were never built, or if so, were underwater.

Comes now, then, this Commodore Stoltz, who had put up a dazzling hotel in Miami Beach, Florida. He looked over the far-reaching beautiful nursery, promptly bought it, and announced he would here top the magnificence of his fifteen-storey Miami Beach hotel. He broke ground in the late winter and in the following months laid down a branch line to the nearest railroad to haul in the sand and girder work and so on. He was ploughing under the land beyond the plantation house throughout the summer and was just about to raze that lovely little mansion when, in September, God or Nature took a hand. Southern Florida was hit by the most devastating hurricane in its history. The Commodore's Miami Beach masterpiece – all fifteen storeys and its hundred-foot radio tower – was demolished. (The only club he was commodore of was his hotel.) Mr Stoltz filed for bankruptcy. It was the end of his hopes for a Stoltz hotel chain.

So there lay in the hands of a holding company, abandoned, and, after the Wall Street Crash of 1929, abandoned and unsold, the three hundred and sixty-five acres with such a colourful history. Who would redeem them and leave us with what we have today: the most beautiful inland course on earth? Enter one Cliff Roberts, a young high school drop-out, a travelling salesman who got into oil leases and, in the late 1920s, was described in the financial papers as 'the wizard of Wall Street'. His wizardry, though badly dented by the Crash, had not deserted him. He had been in the habit of going to Augusta in the winter to play golf and stay at a local hotel where, from time to time, stayed a young lawyer – the now immortal Robert Tyre (Bobby) Jones, the world's leading golfer, who, having conquered all four majors in one year and still an amateur, promptly retired at the age of 28. Mr Roberts ran into him in Augusta. Very soon, Mr Roberts learned from Jones that he had one ambition left: to design his own golf course. Tapping what in those days they called 'contacts' for money was right up Mr Roberts' alley. He also had a nose for sniffing out pieces of obscure real estate that might be bought at Depression prices. He spotted the abandoned Fruitlands. First he quietly collected the capital from his, well, capitalist, friends and one day he led Jones to the gates of the property. They drove up the magnolia drive to the plantation house (which God, the hurricane and the Commodore's bankruptcy had left intact). Bobby Jones walked through the house onto the terrace where stood, and stands, a gnarled monumental live oak tree. He looked beyond what is now the long cathedral sweep of the tenth fairway and shifted his gaze across to Rae's Creek, the little bridge and the glistening water. 'This', said Jones, 'is the place.' And so it was. And so it is.

I've talked about it, and how it came about,

because many of you – golfers or not, wherever you are, in Britain, Australia, Japan even – can get some sense of its peculiar beauty this Sunday afternoon or evening – 13 April – 'the cruellest month', the poet said, 'mixing memory and desire'. Well, for me certainly, many memories. I mentioned that I am not, will not be, there this year – for an inevitable, rather chilling reason that never crossed my mind when I enthusiastically booked my motel room months ago. All my playmates, the guys I walked the course with, dined and drank and reminisced with – Pat Ward-Thomas and Leonard Crawley and Henry Longhurst and Peter Dobreiner, and other great men you've never heard of – they're all gone. It occurred to me rather late in the day that I'd be parting with a lot of dollars to fly seven hundred miles south for the privilege of dining alone in the motel. Anyway, we hear that they had a long early spasm of heat a week or more ago, and for the first time in many, many years, all the blooms are gone. Tragic. So, as it is, here I am in New York with my old friend (once a playing partner) and the barley wine, and the magical new telly with the better-than-a-movie image (forget digital), and my wife, who, after fifty years and getting to like the looks of Greg Norman and Freddie Couples, has become an addict.

Summer

The Summer Bachelor

16 June 1950

An American telephoned me the other day to ask me
what was meant by 'flannelled fools'. I had to explain
to him that in Britain the summer game is played in
flannels. He jumped, wrongly, to the conclusion that
boxing was the British summer pastime and that everybody got fitted out for it in long skiing underwear. I
introduced him gently to some of the mysteries of
cricket, not the least of which is why grown men stand
around for most of the day doing nothing at all in
temperatures of 50 degrees. I tried to keep my expo-
sition to simple words, but when you are talking about
transatlantic weather the simplest words are the most
deceiving. I remember once picking up the Paris
edition of the New York *Herald Tribune* and looking
up to the left-hand corner of the front page to see
how the people were faring in the Manhattan midsum-
mer. It prints the weather report of London, Paris and
New York, and the newspaper naturally has to take
on trust the language of the weather bureau of origin.
It said, 'London, fair, 71 degrees, continued hot; Paris,

78, warm; New York, clear, high 83, seasonably cool.'

This could serve as a text for the British export drive, which falters always on the presumption that an American means the same thing as an Englishman when he talks of a 'light suit'. In Britain, it appears to mean light in colour. Here it means light-weight. If this is understood, the golden rule for the textile exporter will then be clear: it is to coax the American buyer into purchasing large quantities of the raw material in Britain – as sheep, if you like – and then let him use it and cut it according to his habits and his needs. For British clothes in America will make a man feel uncomfortable outdoors in summer and indoors in winter. It is possible for a North European to feel at home here any time up to Christmas. He could keep his old habits and his regular suits and feel he was still in a temperate climate. The New Year transports him to the pole, and in a temperature of one above (above zero, that is) the word 'cold' will take on a sharper meaning for a Londoner, say, who has never in his or his forebears' lifetime known anything colder than 9 degrees. Summer here is, however, the bigger problem for the Briton. He is rightly aware that New York is named after old York but he goes on to the fatal assumption that the trip from one to the other involves a direct east-to-west passage of three thousand miles. What he rarely knows is that he has also gone eight hundred miles south, that old York is located on a level with the tundra of Labrador, whereas New York is at the precise latitude of Corfu.

This clash between the romantic legend of our sameness and the facts of life is what sparks the Englishman's shock. He discovers that the changeover from winter to summer life is brutally abrupt, and that to adjust to the violent swing of the thermometer he has to acquire habits more suited to a fieldhand in a banana republic than to the gentle vagaries of a London heatwave. (I recall another London headline: '75 Again Today! No Relief in Sight.') He will discover that New York is more of a summer furnace than a summer festival. He will learn that it has created unfamiliar local institutions. He will soon hear about the summer bachelor, the forgotten man of American folklore.

To appreciate the pathos and charm of the summer bachelor, you have to learn the stages by which a normally jogging and contented husband becomes one. Last week, then, the family took off for our summer house at the end of Long Island. (This is a custom not restricted to what used to be called the upper-middle class. The continental mainland of the United States sweats abominably from May to October and any humane husband who is not fettered to the marriage bed will rent a shack anywhere in the mountains, by a lake or a seashore, as far as possible from Chicago, St Louis, Pittsburgh or a score of other infernos.) The induction into summer bachelorhood is almost as violent as the season that causes it. One day you are living in a normal house or apartment, with carpets, grocery deliveries, timed meals, friends and everything; and the next you'd think the Russians were coming. Your wife is out of bed like a rocket. She beats around the house like a beaver. 'Excuse me,' she says, as I am in the middle of a shrewd sentence on the typewriter, and up comes the carpet. Up come all the carpets. At 10 a.m. the kitchen doorbell buzzes and a huge man in an apron clomps in and, with the aid of three helpers, lugs the carpets away to be stored.

There is a clatter of china in the kitchen. All the civilized eating utensils are going into boxes and cocoons of tissue paper. My wife breaks in again and lifts a warning finger. She indicates one shelf and one drawer. 'There you are,' she says. For the next three months or more I am to use two cracked kitchen plates, a chipped saucer, drink my coffee out of a premature Coronation mug (Edward VIII) and stir it with a spoon bought fifty years ago by her mother, a relentless Southerner. It looks like a petrified alligator, and that is what it's meant to look like. It says on it, 'A present from Jacksonville, Florida'.

Now there is a noise not unlike the furious exhaust that sets in at the tenser moments of science-horror movies ('The radio-isotope, Fleming, throw the safety rod, man!'). It is a team of vacuum cleaners. I stumble into the living room, for it is in darkness. The curtains have come down and four shades have gone up, two white ones on the outside, two green ones inside. The nifty satin upholstery on the sofa is obscured by a dingy slipcover. So are all the upholstered chairs. The lamps are swathed in bedsheets, giving them the appearance of Arab sentinels. A screen is being pulled across the open entrance to the living room, and my wife gives the annual order: 'Stay out of here, remember!' (I have no theories about American wives. They are, so far as I'm concerned, wives.) A mountain of laundry is piling up in the hall. There is a tearing sound coming from the clothes closets – the winter clothes are being entombed in plastic hangers and all the clothes give off a characteristic smell. It used to be mothballs. You used to hear them rattle around in the night. Now they tinkle, for they roll up and down small perforated tins with hooks on them that hang on the racks. The closets are squirted with some noxious chemical, and the ones that contain the winter suits are dynamited with bombs of DDT. This may all sound very drastic. Alas, our insidious summer enemy is a beast unknown to a true temperate climate – the buffalo moth – and if you ignore him, you are apt to confront an interesting wardrobe in the fall, of garments that might have served as targets on a rifle range.

So now, the blankets are entombed, the sheets changed, rooms closed off, refrigerator defrosted and denuded of food (it looks neater that way, to my wife at least, when she returns in October). I am permitted to run the refrigerator sometime later and it will soon contain tins of beer, a mouldy tomato, a box of crackers, and some limes and lemons. Just before the family leaves, she issues the battle orders for the summer campaign: 'Always put the garbage out before you go to bed, never start on a new bottle of milk before you've finished the old one. Never go out and leave the windows open. Keep the shades drawn in the living room. Right?' Very good, General, and goodbye.

The winter cycle is completed the summers that the children go to camp. There is a special fuss to be made with duffel bags and blankets and swimming shorts and two blankets and name tapes. And you all go off to Grand Central Station and align your brood with one of the many regiments of children lined up and waiting for the call to their track and their train. And again you hear one of the most powerful folk songs of America. A stationmaster stands by a large board and he looks at a card in his hand that lists all the names of the camps and the platforms of their outgoing trains. Nine-thirty strikes. And he warms up his baritone and chants: 'Indian Summer – track nineteen. Shining Mountain – seventeen. Pine Grove – twenty-one. Camp Wawokeewe – nine. High Wind – fifteen. Meadow Lark – eighteen. Thunderbolt – twenty-nine.'

It is over. They are gone. You leap to a telephone and locate another displaced person. You bathe and shave and hear yourself singing forgotten songs of liberation. This first evening is unusually high-spirited. The drinks flow free and so does the coarse interchange of remarks about family life. You decide that your companion is a fine man you have tended to underestimate. Then you go home and recall with a start that you are on your own again. You hear your shoes crackle on the dust of the desert that is the long, dark hall. You peek into the living room and switch on a light. The standing lamp by the switch is a dim figure indeed. Its shade has been wrapped around with a fez of crinkly white paper, and it stands there like Lawrence of Arabia in ambush. You duck out and into the bedroom. The silence is chilling. You get a beer and read a little, or stay up and watch the late show, and then the late late show. At three you turn in, and at eight you feel terrible. Each weekend, you suffer the troop trains of the New Haven or Long Island Railroad and limp raggedly into the bosom of your family. On Monday it starts again.

At this point a suspicion will have crossed your mind that has certainly crossed the mind of the summer bachelor. Indeed, George Axelrod made a play about it and called it *The Seven Year Itch*. The title itself suggests a clinical thesis and we will leave it with its author. For most men it does not take seven years to recall that New York contains, among its martyred and lonely millions, an old girlfriend, or some agreeable but impeccable social worker, or some other honest female whose devotion to her work denies her the blissful exile your wife is now embarked on. Peter Arno captured and immortalized this suspicion – of yours – in a cartoon that showed a portly gent, one of those waggish Blimps with the spotted bow tie, marching smartly down Park Avenue with a very trig young woman on his arm. Coming up the avenue, and just level with him, is a majestic matron of about his age. 'Why, George Fitzgerald,' she cries, 'what*ever* keeps you in town?'

I will not blemish a family programme with any other comment than the thought that one of the most profound of all American idioms is that priceless old catchphrase: 'I love my wife but oh you kid.' I bring up this touchy subject because an accident of technology is, I think, about to produce a sociological revolution in the United States. And I know that you expect me to keep you up with sociological revolutions. The cause of this one is the air conditioner. In the old summer days, the summer bachelor went at weekends from the oven of his apartment to undressed days and what he thought of as cool nights. Now he leaves the ice-cool paradise of his apartment for the hot days and the dank nights and the midges and bugs of the country.

Two days ago, a Wednesday, I pressed the elevator button of my apartment house and as the door slid back it revealed the capacious frame of a neighbour of mine from the twelfth floor. He is a retired old gentleman, a notable fisherman and a solid but saucy character. I asked him what kept *him* in town in mid-week. 'Are you kidding?' he said. 'It's like the basin of the Ganges out there. I retreated to this wonderful apartment. And you know what? My wife showed up this morning. God damn!'

'If this goes on,' I said, 'it's going to play the devil with fishing.'

'Fishing nothing,' he said. 'It's going to play hell with marriage.'

A Letter from Long Island

18 August 1978

As you may have heard, all the New York City newspapers – all three of them – are on strike. How, then, am I going to acquaint you with what is being said, and thought, and speculated about all the great issues of the day? I am not. It may be cold-blooded to say so but this seems to me to offer a golden opportunity to disclaim all responsibility for being well-informed, or informed at all. I could spoil it for you – and for me – by remarking that the television networks are doubling and tripling their coverage from New York and of the local controversies that spring from the strike. So it's possible to sit down at 6 p.m. and emerge four hours later choked and dizzy with facts and fancies.

In the middle of a sweaty August, it seems to me to be a mistake not to make the most of the surcease from the *New York Times*. Far better, I hope you'll agree, if I retreat to where I belong and tell you something about life as it is lived at the end of Long Island.

I don't mean to give you the romantic notion that the end of the Island – we are precisely one hundred miles from door to door – is a romantic haven devoid of all involvement with the modern world. On the contrary, it would be possible for a nosey reporter to make it over into a miniature of the nation's plight.

The county politicians voted not to raise the pay of our local sheriffs, so for a day or two the prison guards called in to say they were all feeling very poorly. Rural crime has increased by 3 per cent in the past year – up in our village from ten robberies to – presumably – ten and a third! There is a mild hulla-baloo about a proposal to build an atomic plant in the middle of our potato fields. The groundwater supply, our only source of water, is becoming polluted with nitrates from fertilizers used by farm-ers and golf clubs, and it's going to cost a quarter of a million dollars to keep the water safe for humans. And so on.

Enough. You must picture the island as a fish, a very long fish with its snout on the left and its tail on the right. Its mouth is hooked to Manhattan and its body reaches into the Atlantic in a direction more easterly than anything, for about one hundred and twenty miles. Its tail is divided into two flukes, which enclose a bay about thirty miles long, five to six miles wide. This is called Peconic Bay (the Peconics were a tribe of Indians, fishermen, whom the refugees from Suffolk came on in the seventeenth century).

There are certain places of the earth I would rather

be than anywhere else, at certain times of the year. In the fall, there is nowhere I would rather be than Vermont, for the beauty of its scarlet and gold landscape – except Long Island, for its shining days and its miraculous draught of fishes. In fact, there is nowhere I know – not the Mediterranean, or the Crimea, most certainly not California – where, between May and November, there is such a succulent haul of so many kinds of splendid eating fish. We are just at the point where the northern coldwater fish nibble at our shores and where the warm-water fish abound. First, for the gourmet, are the noble striped bass, and the bluefish. Then the swordfish, and the flounder, and the lemon sole. But there are also other very tasty species, which city people either don't know about or despise out of genteel ignorance. In the summer months, the fat flat porgy is always mooching along the bed of the bay. It is very easy to catch by bouncing a sinker on the bottom and stirring up enough sand and mud to blind it. It is a paranoid species that feels it's being chased by submarines and so comes to the surface along a zigzag course, as if in convoy during wartime. Baked porgy is delicious, and I simply have no idea why it never appears on restaurant menus.

Then there is the blowfish, known to the local tots as the swell-belly, for the exact reason that when it's grounded it blows itself up like a balloon in the hope of disposing of the hook. It is regarded by weekenders as a pest fish, but it has down its backbone a

slim triangular fillet of firm flesh, the closest thing
we have to the delicious rubbery texture – I'm afraid
there is no other word – of a Dover sole. More
remarkable still is the city's non-acceptance of the
weakfish. I have caught it and savoured it for forty
years. It is so called because it has a weak, papery
mouth, which it cheerfully – I presume – rips in order
to dislodge the hook. It then swims off and grows
its mouth together again. Maybe its name is the snag.
Some years ago, droll Italians who owned fish
markets on the South Shore took to laying out
weakfish and marking them with a sign saying, 'Sea
Trout'. They were out of stock within an hour of
piling up the weaks.

The island, like all other bits of geography, has its
own local lingo for its different districts that will not
be found on maps or in atlases. Thus, the northern
fluke – where I live – is known as the North Fork.
But the southern fluke is known as the South *Shore*
(never mind that some old families over there try to
retain the South Fork). The natives of the North Fork
say they are going 'South Side' whenever they are
disposed to do so, which is not often, for reasons I
hasten to explain.

The South Shore used to be the exclusive mon-
opoly of early Dutch and English landowners. One
of the latter, William Floyd, was a signer of the
Declaration of Independence and achieved a very late
badge of immortality by having a motorway named
after him. The early settlers were a little miffed, at

the end of the nineteenth century, when some of the robber barons and their heirs moved in. One of them, name of Vanderbilt, visited Scotland and saw the natives playing the peculiar game known locally as 'the gowf'. He accordingly imported some clubs, hired a landscape man, or golf architect, and commissioned him to lay out the first twelve-hole links course in the United States.

Until the Second World War, the fashionable resorts of the South Shore – Southampton, Bridgehampton, Easthampton – were pretty choosy places. But following the immemorial custom of all Western societies, the latest batch of the new rich moved as close to the old rich as possible in the hope of having some of their effortless poise brush off on them. In the past twenty or thirty years, these once fussy compounds have been invaded by brokers, interior decorators, bankers, chic painters, actors and actresses, television producers, and infested by tenpercenters of all kinds.

If you detect a note of inverted snobbery in this account, your instinct is correct. I have summered and autumned (fallen?) on the North Fork for forty-two years. We stand out on our hundred-foot high cliff or bluff and look across the five or six miles of the quarantine waters that separate us from the chic, the bad and the beautiful. The North Fork is not chic. It is not rich. I doubt there are more than half a dozen residents whose combined securities could match the portfolio of any one of several hundreds of the denizens of Easthampton and Southampton. The North Fork was for two and a half centuries the province of English settlers from Suffolk, and you can follow the family lines through platoons of tombstones, the victims of seventeenth-century epidemics, and all the wars since the Revolution, in the local graveyards or what – in my village – is known as 'the burying ground'. I know old people, and not so old, who only once in their lifetime have made the hundred-mile trip to New York. They didn't like what they saw, and went no more.

Shortly after the robber barons invaded the South Shore the North Fork was invaded by immigrant Poles: Catholic farmers. Like all immigrants, they had a nostril tuned to the smell of their native soil. And the North Fork, planted as far as the eye can see with potatoes and cauliflower and corn, is interrupted only by a few old colonial churches but more conspicuously by squat wooden churches with blunt spires. The Fork could be used today with great accuracy as the location for a film about central Poland.

The Poles were industrious and very thrifty and in no time took over the big duck farms, which had been run in a comfortable way by the Anglos. So now, our Fork is populated mostly by the descendants of the original English and by third-generation Poles. And in the manner of long-settled rural communities, the North Forkers tend to take a dim view of the South Shore. But then, the South Shore takes no view at all of the North Fork. In fact, friends of ours on the South Side have lived and died there without having the faintest idea where the North Fork was or how to find our point, though it's clearly visible from the Peconic shore of their side. I still have friends who ask us every summer, 'How are things at your place in Southampton?' Which is like asking a proud Lancastrian, 'How are things in Bradford and Leeds?'

Our point is called Nassau Point. After the English occupation it was rechristened Hog's Neck, but it reverted later on to Nassau since, under the Dutch, it had been designated as a sliver of crown property by King William (Prince, you'll recall, of Orange and Nassau). Since then the Point has managed to remain unmentioned in the history books or even in the newspapers. In fact, we are so obscure that when Nassau Point achieved the fame of a new comet, nobody noticed it. It needed no newspaper strike to leave us unhonoured and unsung. But that is another story. Another letter.

Fall

Farewell to San Francisco

18 October 2002

From time to time, an old acquaintance will call me just before I do my talk and say, 'Well, I think we all know what you're going to talk about this week.' I tend to say, 'That's right', or 'You got it', because I know in my bones, from years of such calls, that they haven't got it. It's always about some appalling natural disaster, a fire, an earthquake, perhaps the assassination of a foreign statesman. In any case, I find no occasion for intelligent comment about the lamentable snipings in the Virginia–Maryland country, or about the nightclub bombing on the once island paradise of Bali. The only reaction must be, 'Isn't it awful?' There is nothing useful you or I can do about it, except to add that Bali and, possibly, the snipings miserably confirm our discovery that the explosions of the past few years, from Scotland to the South Pacific, are not the spontaneous outbursts of fanatical loners but the long-prepared world war of a worldwide network called al-Qa'ida.

But now there is a topic which is not to be guessed

at, and was dictated quite simply by my looking at the calendar and reflecting: ah, yes, the third week in October, which has meant for so many years, 'San Francisco time'. Certainly, for the past thirty years or so I have been going four times a year to my favourite city to see how America, its life and affairs, looks from the Pacific Coast.

Visually, the first thing that struck me, from the start, was the Oriental connection. It has been there since the first Chinese labourers were brought in by the Central Pacific Company to work their way east and meet the Irish working west, together to create the first transcontinental railroad. In the middle of the Utah desert in May 1869, two locomotives timidly nosed together, and a lad on a high telegraph pole tapped out for the wonder of the world the message: 'The last rail is laid. The last spike is driven. The Pacific railroad is finished.' That moment has been celebrated in many a sentimental calendar painting with railroad company dignitaries in cutaways banging in a gold spike. A more prosaic, not to say brutal, memory has stayed green in the recollections of the railroad crews and their descendants. Several days before the historic moment, the two grades had run side by side for a stretch, and the Irishmen took such an instant aversion to the little slant-eyed Chinese that they blasted them with dynamite. The Chinese swiftly buried their dead and returned the gesture with pickaxes. The massacre was brief and bloody but the racial feud it brewed simmered throughout the nineteenth century.

By the time I first arrived in San Francisco, just on seventy years ago, Chinatown was the most compact and orderly of all the ethnic settlements. It had a thriving tourist business, and the California–Oriental connection was strong and detectable everywhere, from the old Chinese in the early morning on Nob Hill doing their slow-motion graceful exercises, to the furniture, porcelain, murals and other Chinese decorations in friends' houses and in hotels. Just along the block from the first hotel I ever stayed in was a glittering metallic statue of Sun Yat Sen, for many decades a cult figure among Californians. He had been a revolutionary who overthrew the last dynasty and was the first President of a Chinese republic.

By the late 1930s, China, overrun by the Japanese in Manchuria, had become California's favourite victim state. However, at that time the ranking villain to Californians as well as to all other Americans was Adolf Hitler. Only experts at the State Department worried about Japan. Only experts, and one Californian, William Randolph Hearst, a national newspaper tycoon, who sat in his castle looking across the Pacific and rang editorial alarm bells warning about the Yellow Peril, about an actual threat of the Japanese to the security, to the shores, of his beloved California.

To visiting Easterners and Europeans, these foaming outbursts were always thought fanciful to the point of absurdity – until 7 December 1941, when out of the blue the Japanese destroyed half the United

States Pacific Fleet (and its air arm) at its base in the Pacific, which most Americans, or for that matter ranking members of the British Embassy (and yours truly) had never heard of. It was called Pearl Harbor.

By now, of course, everything has gone into reverse. Japan is, has been, the great modern trading partner, and China, though vilified and warily watched since it went Communist, is being wooed as the second largest Pacific trader. But in San Francisco, the Oriental, or as we must now say the Asian, presence is as triumphant as anywhere in the country. A medical office building I know which twenty, thirty years ago was inhabited by doctors with American-European names now has a third of its tenants Asian. They are refugees from the Communist takeover of Vietnam, or Hong Kong Chinese whose parents came to this country, say twenty-five years ago, without a word of English. Today, they are young medical specialists.

These things I shall miss, but most of all the daily sights and sounds that are San Francisco and nowhere else. First, of course, the nine tumbling hills, and how remarkably the people troop up and down them like one of the great race migrations of the Middle Ages. The white city is seen from across the bay as a vast pyramid of confetti. The genial sun most of the year, the bafflement verging on outrage of the summer tourists shivering atop a hilly street, not having been told that July and August are the coldest months. But summer is memorable also for the arrival from the

Pacific in the late afternoon of great plumes of white fog moving in on the city with the motion of a slow freight train. The double moan of the foghorn at night. The deceptively blue waters under the Golden Gate Bridge in whose icy, thrashing currents no Alcatraz escapee has ever been known to survive, only the corpse of one Aaron Burgett.

Over and over again, I recall a short piece of Mark Twain's which says so much about San Francisco in so little. It reports Mark Twain's arrival in San Francisco after he'd been thrown out of the silver-mining town of Virginia City, Nevada, for having written that 'in this noble city, there are two churches and seventy-six saloons – which is just about the right proportion'. This line aroused such fury in the local church matrons that Mark Twain thought it was time 'to get lost – so I absquatulated.'

After the sagebrush and alkali desert of Nevada, San Francisco was heaven on the half shell. I lived at the best hotel. I exhibited my clothes in the most conspicuous places. I infested the opera.

I enjoyed my first earthquake. It was just after noon on a bright Sunday in October and I was coming down Third Street . . . As I turned a corner there came a terrific shock . . . the entire front of a four-story brick building sprung outward like a door and fell sprawling across the street. The ground rolled under me in waves. The streetcars stopped. Their horses were rearing and plunging. Every door of every house was vomiting a stream of human beings . . .

The first shock brought down two or three organ pipes in one of the churches, and the next instant, in the atmosphere where the minister had stood, there was a vacancy. In another church, after the first shock, the minister said: 'Bretheren, keep your seats. There is no better place to die than here.' After the third shock, he waved his flock goodbye and added: 'But outside is good enough for me.'

After a time, I had to cease being an onlooker at the peculiar life of San Francisco and get down to earning a livelihood. My first job was with the *Enquirer*, and my first assignment was accidental: a set-to between a Chinaman and some Irish. Now, the Chinese are a harmless race when white men let them alone or treat them no worse than dogs. Their chief employment is to wash clothes, which they do at low prices with their usual patience and industry. One day, I saw a bunch of Irish toughs descend on an old Chinaman, on his way home after laundering the clothes of his Christian clientele. They sat on him and beat him up. I went back to the office in a state of high indignation and wrote my fill of this miserable incident. But the editor refused to print it. Our paper, he said, was printed for the poor, and in San Francisco the Irish *were* the poor. In time, I cooled off. I was lofty in those days. I have survived.

Most poignantly I recall and miss most a contemporary – long gone – writer, a columnist for the San Francisco morning paper. I often wonder if San Franciscans deserved him, for he never received any special tribute as the best writer ever to come out of that city. His name was Charles McCabe, a funny, beautiful writer of great simplicity, by which I mean he felt deeply and thought clearly. He was never syndicated outside that one paper. 'Why not?' I once asked the editor. 'Well,' he said, 'who's going to buy a man who's more of a meditator than a columnist?' It's true. One day he wrote about the pain of being jilted, next day on Cicero, next a dangerously funny swipe at the women's libbers, next day the life of St Thomas Aquinas.

McCabe looked like a giant, dignified W. C. Fields with a similarly glowing nose. It came at you like a beacon, but before you sighted it your nostrils picked up the unmistakable odour of 'the poteen'. At the end of his life, Charlie McCabe became aware of the one thing that makes any life worth living. 'These days the love I give and the love I get seems spread around rather thin. I am often lonely but seldom bored any more. There's a lot of peace and quiet but I now know it would not be possible without friends. Without friends? I can hardly bear to think about it.' Nor can I.

They are the San Franciscans it will hurt to miss.

The Fall of New England

21 October 1949

There are times of the year when anybody with an itch for travel must think of those parts of the earth that God favoured above all others when He handed out the seasons. There are two of these that I have enjoyed many times but I still find myself goggling and marvelling every time they come around. One is the English spring and the other is New England in the fall.

The best of English poets have celebrated the rich, sombre English autumn, but an American fall bears little resemblance to that 'season of mists and mellow fruitfulness'. Many famous Britons have put on record their astonishment at the youthful, trumpeting quality of the fall, at the hot days and the Mediterranean blue skies encircling a landscape of blinding scarlet and gold. Lord Bryce, not a reticent man about American vices, couldn't trust his English reserve to speak properly about its virtues. Lloyd George confessed after his only trip to America that no matter how inconclusive his political mission had been he would at least go home remembering the overwhelming experience of the fall. A hundred years ago, Mrs Trollope, who liked very little about these United States, broke down and wrote that at this season of the year 'the whole country goes to glory'.

The fall ranges throughout the whole hardwood or deciduous region of the country, from the north woods of Maine clear across the Midwest as far as the Dakotas and way down South to the foothills of the Rockies in Texas. Since no American can bear to believe that her or his parents chose a second-rate place to be born in, there is no agreement about where the fall is at its best. The residents of the Great Lakes say that no sumacs flame like their sumacs. And the pride of a man from Arkansas in his blazing hawthorn trees is a wild grab at plucking a virtue out of necessity. A native of another land can simply report that the fall of New England is as a four-alarm fire to a lighted match. There is no way to describe it or talk about it, except in the language of Milton and Shakespeare, who never saw it.

But it is possible to say why it's so. Everybody enthuses about the fall but nobody explains it. It is due to a happy accident of climate, a steady brilliance of October sun going to work on the great variety of American hardwoods and the fairly arid soil they stand in. The superiority of New England's fall – of that in Vermont, New Hampshire and Massachusetts especially – is due to their latitude. These states are far enough north to get an early cold spell to quicken the sap before the prolonged sunshine of October brings it out as colour in the leaves. They are far enough south to escape a continuous and withering frost, which is what nips the Canadian fall before it can come to its prime. Farther south – in Pennsylvania, Maryland, Virginia and the Carolinas – they get no cold, except at high altitudes, and by the time the sap is forced up and ready for showing off, the leaves are crumbling and falling.

In most temperate countries the strong pigments that have been hidden from view in the greens of summer never do come out, because the autumn brings in rain and mists and threatening grey skies. The whole trick of the New England fall is nothing more complicated than that of a photographic negative handled by a superior developer. In the autumn, the countrymen tell us, the sap is blocked from the leaf by a new growth of hard cells at the base of the twig. So the greens fade. Now all you need is an October of brilliant light and warmth to develop out the yellows and the reds. The only other qualification is a lack of rain. On rich and rainy soils like those of England the leaves stay green too late till the frost kills them. New England, on the contrary, has many causes to lament its rather poor soils. But it never regrets them in the fall, for their very lack of nitrogen stimulates a great range of yellows and golds. And the acid in the leaves is what burns them scarlet. The fall, then, is nothing more than the thorough burning out of what is poor in the soil and what is bitter in the leaf. 'It is,' says Donald Culcross Peattie, 'essentially death that causes all the brave show.' But it is a fierce and productive death.

I once went north from New York City at the very beginning of the fall to meet the peak of it wherever it might be between Maine and southern Connecticut. The first signal of the glory to come is a bare tree, which is never bare until the fall is ready to ripen. It is the butternut tree, and it sheds everything just as the bushes and berries are beginning to trickle out their purple. By the green edge of the parkway on which I was driving, little piles of brown leaves, already dead, lay at the foot of hickory trees. The ferns were dry. The bracken and blueberry bushes were wine-dark, the sumac a throbbing vermilion. Everywhere there was the smell of burning wood, letting off violet wisps of smoke to smear the cloudless sky – like trickles of milk on window panes.

At this point I wanted to take off my glasses, which a notation on my driving licence forbids. This is another thing about the fall. The sparkling clarity of the light gives to short-sighted people the constant sense that their eyesight has marvellously improved and that they are seeing fences, barns, steeples and billboards in the sharp outline they probably have for other people all the time.

I drove up and over the hills across from New York State into Connecticut, past roadside stands piled high with jugs of cider and pyramids of pumpkins. And then I started to follow a river whose banks were black with stands of evergreen. By now a green field was just another daub on the crowded palette of the landscape. We were still far from the fall's peak. It was still the small, treeless things that were trying to be splendid. The briar and bushes and vines were sparkling. I do not know them well enough to single out their separate charms, but it is an annual joy to see brush which most of the time is a mesh of old wire suddenly disclose a jewel of a flower. Pokeweed, and pitchpine cone, and unpretentious things like partridge berry and jack-in-the-pulpit. All of them have a special shining berry, a bursting husk, a momentary bloom.

I got out of the car and wallowed in the silence and the singing colour and the balmy heat. At the rim of my tyre I noticed that the smooth white cement of the highway had cracked under the tension of a cranberry vine. And through this crack, and edging into the highway, wild cranberries grew. I looked ahead at the engineered boulevard of the highway, pouring like two ribbons of toothpaste to the horizon, quite heedless of its defeat by the concentrated violence of a tiny and delicate vine. That just about put industrial know-how in its proper place. And I climbed back and went on, warming to the excitement of what was to come.

And now the trees took over. After another twenty miles, the evergreens came in thick and fast. Even a pine looked like a new invention seen in its inkiness against a flaming maple. Now I was surrounded by two other properties that make the New England fall unique. First and above all the maple, with its bursting sugar which blazes into scarlet. And then the oaks. An Englishman is surprised to wonder about many slender trees and hear them called oaks. The fat old oak tree of England, with his legs planted solidly on lush damp ground, is a rare sight. But New England has a teeming variety of oaks, and their value as a spectacle is that in the fall they entirely revise your ideas about the infinite fine range of colour between gold and lemon. And beside this perpetual shower of scarlet and lemon and gold, the white birches slid by like slivers of mercury. And rising from the foam of every valley, slim as thermometers, were the white spires of colonial churches, keeping count of the general fever. I had hit the peak, and the state of our language being what it is, in my hands at least, there is no more point in going on about it in prose. Some great composer might convey the majesty of it. Only a child in ecstasy could hit off the youth and hilarity of it. For children are natural impressionists, taking the adjectives of music and knifing them close against the nouns of sight and touch. Every child knows that colour sings and trees walk. But puberty is the end. They acquire the logic that is death to the spirit and life to what is called maturity, and like the rest of us repress the wild energy of their instinctive knowledge. And so we can only guess at the form of art in which perhaps some hundreds of years from now the New England fall will come to be represented. I would take a bet that, by our present resources, Cézanne and Handel together might give a fair account of it. For the present I can only tell you that the fall is wonderful in life and awful in painting.

In this setting you can find an American life, proud but not prosperous, that also seems doomed to die in the industrial democracy that surrounds it. Don't imagine that the small village I am taking you into, in the south of Vermont, is typical of New England today. It is typical of nowhere else, but New England is many things besides small memorials to the declining eight-eenth century. The New England puritan of English stock has not been the typical New Englander for two generations. Sixty per cent of the people in the six states of New England have at least one parent foreign born, against only 5 per cent in the Southern states. Today the Connecticut Yankee has only one chance in three of being, like the first settlers, a Protestant with an English name. It's two to one that he's an Italian or a Pole, and a wise newspaper editor once warned me to take for granted that any stranger I met on the streets of New England was a Catholic. To make certain that what I am going to talk about, though once radical and typical in New England, is now conservative and odd, I should also warn you that the typical Yankee is no longer a farmer. In 1790, ninety-seven New Englanders in every hundred lived on the land, and three in towns. In 1870, it was still only twenty-one townsfolk against seventy-nine countrymen. Today in the United States, 56 per cent of the people live in cities. In New England, 77 per cent of the entire population lives in cities, only 23 per cent in the country. So New England is the most industrialized of all American regions. If this shocks you, it would shock most Americans more, for they stubbornly think back to New England as the source and replenisher of all their canniest and most down-to-earth virtues.

Bearing in mind, then, that we are looking at a tiny green spot in the upper-right-hand corner of the turbulent industrial landscape of the northeastern states, let's take a look at the sort of place that bred New England. It is a small valley six miles long and two miles wide. You might say that it was bound by mountains, but to a Westerner they would be low, well-wooded hills, for the hills that enclose this valley are nowhere higher than a thousand feet. Yet the valley is more fertile than most places in Vermont, with grass for summer pasture and winter hay. It grows corn and perhaps a crop of oats. And the farmer's cash in the bank comes from the one cow a year he sells. To a stranger it would look like good sheep country, and so it would be if there weren't out West the vast hills of Montana and Wyoming and Colorado to make it hardly worthwhile for a Vermonter to breed them. Then, there's so much rock and boulder in the hills of Vermont that by now the oldest Vermont joke tells how the sheep have their noses sharpened so they can get at the grass (God anticipated the plight of Vermont by making sheep with cleft lips).

If you were to motor along this valley, and your car had some sort of trouble, a quiet, hard-bitten Vermonter would in time – his time – appear and tinker awhile and in the end put it right. He wouldn't say a word. And you'd have to be an outlander to try and pay him in any way. For Vermonters, settled long ago on a poor soil, and used to winters that hold more snow than the Arctic, don't expect a smiling face from Nature and don't reflect it in themselves.

An Englishman coming here and going straight to
Vermont and expecting to meet casual, backslapping
people would be in for a ghastly surprise. A man is
a stranger there up to the third and fourth genera-
tion. And the only reliable way they have of placing
a face or a name is to ask who his mother was. (His
father simply served his mother's turn.) It's been said
that Vermonters look on life as a necessary struggle
against evil, a struggle you must make and expect to
lose. It's also the only state in the United States where
you will hear the word 'thrift' used all the time. They
never throw anything away. In a little booklet about
this valley I am talking about, written by a couple of
natives, you will read this sentence: 'The people are
friendly and always willing to help a neighbor. This
means more to us who live here than material wealth,
which none of us possess.' To walk into the centre
of this village of Newfane, you would never believe
it. It is a handsome common with a couple of shops,
an inn and a quite magnificent courthouse. The town
was settled in 1776, but the county courthouse didn't
go up until fifty years later, and we can be thankful
for that. For in the interval Americans conceived a
passion for everything Greek. Believing that they had
just successfully established the first genuine democracy since the Greeks and the grandest Republic since
Rome, they took to naming their town with classical
names. Hence Philadelphia, Annapolis, Laconia,
Athens, Sparta, Seneca, Cicero, Troy. Thomas Jefferson
built a home with a columned portico. And soon

country courts, and inns, and farmhouses were doing the same. It may sound like a dubious fad, but Americans stuck to their preference for wooden houses, and today New England is glorified with hundreds of churches, houses, courthouses, the wood painted white, with pillared porticoes and graceful spires. In this small village in Vermont, the county courthouse is an exquisite symbol of what Americans did in wood with Greek forms.

Opposite the courthouse is the inn, which is also the jail. Newfane has kept up its habit of feeding its prisoners from the inn, and since the inn serves the best food around here, it's sometimes hard to get the inmates out of jail. Theodore Roosevelt said he would like to retire here, commit some 'mild crime' and eat his way through a cheerful old age.

If you went along the valley you would be walking without knowing it through another town called Brookline, for Brookline is simply the scattered houses of the valley. It has less than a hundred people, mostly farmers, and they are their own rulers. Its first town meeting was held in 1795 and the last one was held last week. The names at the first meeting are still there: Moore and Waters, and Ebenezer Wellman and Cyrus Whitecomb, and Christopher Osgood (there has always been a Christopher on the Osgood farm). Walking along the road you might run into the tractor of a Mr Hoyt. He is to all intents a farmer. And so he is. He is also the road commissioner of the valley. His wife, Minnie Hoyt, is the town clerk, a justice of the peace, and when she isn't doing the farming chores she's busy signing fishing licences, or marrying a visiting couple, or telling the comfortable city-people who have made a summer home here that by a decision made at the last town meeting their taxes will be twice as much next year. What is striking to an Englishman here is that the few fairly well-to-do people are all what they call 'summer folks', people who made a farm over as a summer retreat from New York or Boston. But the summer folks are strangers and underlings. The valley has heard many delicate sounds through the years. But it has never heard the advice of a squire or the accent of *noblesse oblige*. The farmers are ruled and rulers. The wealthy stranger goes cap in hand and pays his rates according to Minnie Hoyt and does what Mr Hoyt says to keep his part of the highway safe and sound.

Our pilgrimage ends with an odd little building, a round schoolhouse. It was put up in the 1820s and is shaped like a silo, just one room with five windows equally spaced in a circle around it. It was so built, they say, because at that time the valley lived in fear of a highwayman called 'Thunderbolt', whom no one had ever seen. The schoolmaster, a Scot from Muirkirk, one Dr Wilson, had his desk facing the door and could see through all the windows the first approach of any robber, or of the dreaded Thunderbolt. Thunderbolt's presence seemed to have haunted the valley for a couple of decades, but one gets a reassuring picture of Yankee vigilance in the dour figure of Dr Wilson, spelling out his lessons to the valley children and in the twilight letting his fingers play on the barrel of his shotgun as his protective eye rolled around the five windows.

I leave you with this comforting image of the rude forefathers of today's New Englanders. Having led you so far into a mystery, though, it occurs to me you may wonder if they ever caught Thunderbolt. Yes, they did.

When the good Dr Wilson died they took off the high scarf he always wore and on his neck they saw scars and the marks of chains. Sure enough, *he* was Thunderbolt.

Winter

Park Avenue's Colourful Christmas

24 December 1999

The curious thing about a city that boasts extravagantly about its best features, as well as some of its worst, is that there is a never-mentioned little miracle in New York City. It is the railed-off plots of grass that for almost three miles run down the middle of Park Avenue and divide the uptown and downtown traffic. Along this whole stretch (fifty-four blocks from 96th to 42nd Street), what is a constant delight and surprise is the regularly changing character of these more than fifty little gardens. And they're not so little: each, one city block long and about fifteen feet wide.

You drive down this avenue one season of the year through a great ripple of crocuses. Another time, tulips from here to infinity. Sometimes you notice that at each end of each garden there is a new young tree, a hundred or so of them from the 96th Street entrance down to where the Avenue ends at Grand Central Station. Or maybe next time, they are locusts or London plane trees. At Christmas time, as now, they've been replaced by small firs.

I suppose we take it so easily for granted (and thousands of the true city types never notice the changes at all) because the very large workforce that performs these magical transformations works by night and by stealth. In fifty years of living round the corner from this long divide of Park Avenue I have never seen any of them at their remarkable labour of creating, along three miles, complete variations of miniature landscapes about, it seems, once every few weeks.

I know they're at it, because I once tactfully guessed at the fortune it requires to employ them and to maintain this city perquisite. I happened to know the possessor of the fortune, a lady named Mary Lasker (heiress of an advertising multi-millionaire, a self-effacing, absolutely non-socialite doer of many unadvertised good works of which the Park Avenue divider is the only conspicuous one). At Christmas time, especially, it makes me think again, with gratitude, of the late Mary Lasker. For now each tree, a hundred or so, is lit at twilight.

By Mrs Lasker's request, and, thank God, this confirming dictate of the Park Avenue property owners, the trees are not gaily decorated with red bulbs and green bulbs and purple bulbs and yellow bulbs – illuminations that make so many city squares and streets look like amusement arcades gone berserk. Each of the Park Avenue firs is decorated with about five hundred tiny oyster-white bulbs. So at twilight, you look down from the small eminence of 96th Street at this three-mile stretch of small, small fountains of light. All the way down, the only colours are the alternating reds and greens of the traffic lights at the fifty-odd intersections. Now, by day it used to be that the long canyon of Park Avenue was majestically closed at the southern end by the great gold dome of Grand Central Station. Then they built behind it a towering, flat monolith of a skyscraper which blotted out the dome (or indeed the outline) of Grand Central. This defiling obstacle tower has been ingeniously made to evaporate by the night – at Christmas time. As the dark comes on, and both Grand Central and the monolith behind it fade into the black sky, there appears by magic a great white cross. This is achieved by leaving on the lights of so many offices on one floor to form the horizontal bar and many more offices to form the vertical bar.

Simple and sublime; but in the past year or two, I'm afraid, it's been an object of sporadic controversy. From whom? From that fervent bank of First Amendment protestors who sometimes sound as if there were no other clauses in the Bill of Rights: 'Congress shall make no law respecting an establishment of religion.' This has been taken in many court appeals in many states to forbid every expression of any religion – by word, decorating, symbol – on *public* property. This argument has been going on for years and years and is effectively won, mainly in places where agnostics or atheists speak louder and longer than the true believers in any religion popular in a given town. So far, by the way, there have been no protests against the dozen performances of *Messiah* and a half-dozen of Bach's *Christmas Oratorio*, even done in public auditoriums or theatres. The board of ACLU (the American Civil Liberties Union) appears to be slipping.

There are some states, however, that can afford to be more blasé or unintimidated by the First Amendment fanatics, for an interesting *new* reason. What is it that Florida, Texas and California have in common that favourably affects the practice of the Christian religion and, say, tends to discourage the march of an army of atheists with banners? The answer: they are the states (Southwestern states) into which more South and Central American immigrants have arrived in the past quarter-century than in the rest of the country put together, the vast majority of them practising Roman Catholics. What they have brought to Christmas is a colourful and quite different tradition of Christmas decoration. Whereas most of the United States picked up the English nineteenth-century trimmings – Prince Albert's Christmas tree, holly and ivy, green and red and so forth, while Britain picked up from New York (via the Dutch settlers) the idea, the well-known figure, of Santa Claus – the Mexicans especially have given us the most colourful and original variations. This week, the Governor of Texas, one George W. Bush, gave a little television tour of the Governor's mansion and showed off a marvellous array of Christmas trees – cacti and pepper trees – hung with orange, and pink flowers and home-made Christmas cribs that looked as if they had been imported from that first Christian (Coptic) chapel outside Cairo, which has those primitive, comic-strip figures of Adam and Eve and a jolly snake. But here in Austin, Texas, were all the nativity figures: the Wise Men, Joseph and Mary, the shepherds, as marvellous little painted wooden figures which we (the civilized Anglo-European types who couldn't draw a broomstick) call 'primitives'.

Governor Bush, you may have heard, is running for President, and running very hard (the election is only nine months away). And he showed off the delightful Mexican decorations with understandable effusiveness, stopping from time to time to talk in Spanish to a passing child. The public, of course, can visit the Governor's mansion, just as the public makes daily tours of the White House. Incidentally, I ought to throw in that anyone running for public office, for state office anyway, in Florida, Texas, Nevada, Southern California nowadays had better speak Spanish as well as English if he/she holds any hope of being elected.

But whatever variations different immigrant groups may bring in, there is one symbolic expression of Christmas, one that dependably returns every year to appear in theatrical form in city theatres and centres, on national television in half a dozen versions, and is at the moment dazzling nightly audiences in New York City's vast Radio City Music Hall. It is Charles Dickens' *A Christmas Carol*. And the booksellers, including the titans online, indicate that every year the sales of *A Christmas Carol* go smartly up. (Poor Dickens, who lost £200 on the book, sued an outrageous couple who pirated his work and sold it cheaply. He was awarded £1,500 damages, so the couple declared bankruptcy, and Dickens got nothing but had to pay out £700 for his own court fees.)

I suppose that we, for the most of the century, have thought of the *Carol* as the most vivid representation of an old English tradition of Christmas: the feasting and the carolling and Christmas cards and the parties with their particular customs, the tree, the pudding, the kissing and dancing and general merriment. Nothing could be more untrue. For centuries, Christmas was an annual street brawl with a reputation for debauchery and general rowdiness. The Church of England and the Puritans here prohibited it as a religious ceremony (or a celebration of Christ's birth) until well into the eighteenth century. When Dickens published the *Carol* in 1843 nobody had ever seen a Christmas card or a Christmas tree, except at Windsor. The street brawl was still a fact, deplored by respectable people who by then had the custom of taking a half-day off on Christmas Day and holding a special mid-afternoon dinner: the turkey, which had long established himself after his long journey from America, and fowl (I mean game) and pastries, and many, many jellies, and Christmas punch.

When the *Carol* appeared, what delighted everybody was the entertaining, suspenseful plot. But Thackeray said it defied literary criticism. It was a work whose central idea was that Christmas was the paradox of a merry time that entailed duties and obligations, especially to the poor, and added the astonishing new notion that Christmas was a special time of the year for redemption – for everybody to take stock and begin to lead a better life.

It's impossible today to appreciate the shock of this idea disguised as brilliant entertainment. It's at the root of the custom of New Year resolutions. But the wish to make amends for the flaws in one's character is something that some people, a few, become conscious of as they grow old. One was the late, the recently late, actor George C. Scott. Not too long before he died, he gave an engaging, vibrant television interview. He was an engaging, vibrant man. There was much talk about his towering portrayal of General George Patton. When he was asked what his favourite role was, he did not hesitate. George C. Scott was in private life a violent man. It was therefore a surprising and happy thing to hear him say that his favourite role of all was – Ebenezer Scrooge.

Silence in Vermont

29 December 1995

If I were asked what was most memorable about this Christmas, I should have to say an experience unknown to most people in a temperate climate: the experience of absolute silence. I see frowns on the faces of one or two listening friends – and non-friends. And an old P. G. Wodehouse type, a beloved friend, exploding: 'Absolute silence? What absolute twaddle is the man going on about now?'

Well, I was, I am, sitting in a room in a typical white-painted wooden old colonial New England house on a little hilltop in northern Vermont, looking out of high Georgian windows through narrowed eyelids – simply because what I see through the windows is blinding whiteness. A world, a planet of snow rolling away as a white valley, up into the wooded foothills, all the trees having branches like dropping swords of snow, and on beyond up the distant white mountains to, as Johnny Mercer said, a blue umbrella sky.

It is Christmas morning, and the family – the father, the grandmother, the three young girls – have gone off with their mother, who by now, though a year or so short of being a Master (why not Mistress?) of Divinity, is qualified to conduct the service, which she does, and presumably did. Later on, she will have to drive off alone and run a wedding. Tonight, who knows? There may be a death to attend. Mother of five, cook, maid, laundress, bottle-washer, divinity student, workaholic, she yet enjoys what amounts to, in unpredictability, the life of a doctor on call. Tonight, we shall have the goose or turkey or what-ever, and the pudding is already in the pot ready for the steaming – my mother's recipe, amended and elaborated down the years, and soon to have the amendment of a swill of brandy, an addition that would have sent my dear Wesleyan mother into intensive care. On Christmas Day alone, my daughter will have driven in all about a hundred and twenty miles. Someone may say, through all that snow? They've had over forty inches in three weeks. No, not *through*. No wonder the highest tax bite on Vermonters is for road maintenance. In winter, modest snowfall or blizzard alike, you can hear in the middle of the night the snowploughs out – the great huge trucks like moving houses on the federal divided highways (what are known slangily in England as dual carriageways) driving a constant shower of snow high as a waterfall in front of the main plough and depositing it as a continuous high rampart on each side of the highways. The state's own roads have other ploughs, and the county roads the same, and the small climbing hill roads – they too are laboured on by night and day till the storm is done. Truth is, if it was not so, life and work in Vermont (indeed, in more than half the American landscape) would come to a halt. Even then, if you don't have four-wheel drive as well as snow tyres, you are not going anywhere.

So, they went off to church and I, who in my boyhood went without protest to church three times every Sunday, have been indulged in the last few years as a qualified penitent or, perhaps, an old sinner beyond redemption. I stayed home and, as I say, listened to the silence. I will now, for the sake of my P. G. Wodehouse friend, explain what I meant by saying that this experience was one I have not had since I was last up in Vermont at a similar snow-laden white Christmas.

Radio engineers, broadcasters, and perhaps actors will now know what I'm talking about. Indoors, it's any studio that is, as the engineers say, 'dead' – having an acoustical low background noise that only some dogs can hear. Most rooms we all think of as quiet are not so to a recording engineer. He can hear a car changing gears five blocks away. The most unlikely sound crisis I can remember was when we were filming, during *America*, a whole episode about the California Gold Rush. At one point, I was telling about some of the families, the wagon teams, who decided to take a short cut in the California desert and follow the Humboldt River till they'd discovered, too late, that it became a fetid marsh and nothing – a sink. So they had to walk sixty-five miles without water: mules died, so did children, so did some men and women who had, by that time, simply had it. And the survivors, before they mooched on, banged wooden posts in the ground and with a hot poker inscribed a made-up name for an imaginary town because you couldn't write home to Hamburg or Cornwall and say, 'Sorry that your son Jack died nowhere.' It's the most pathetic episode of the Gold Rush, and on an old map you can still see these invented town names. No town was ever there, of course, no building, just the bones of mules and crossed sticks to mark the buried bodies of the unlucky: Endurance, Fortitude, Last Gasp. To film this I walked way off from the crew into the desert till I was a moving midget. The main thing, though, I can tell you stranger: it was mighty quiet. Well, you know, it wasn't. By the time I came into full view and then close up and the scene was on film, the director told me that it looked fine but they could never get silence. The recorder heard a plane or two taking off from an Army Air Force base maybe twenty miles away. The desert was a sounding board. In the event, we kept the picture and put the sound in in a studio in London (England, that is).

Well, I thought on Christmas morning, how I wish I had my old sound men from the *America* crew. They could have filmed and recorded indoors or out. A passing car took about ten seconds to get lost for good and all. After that, the snow provided the 'deadest' studio I'd ever been in. I put my head out the front door – not much more, it was a bright, piping 2 degrees (30 below freezing) – and I talked aloud. I said Good Morning. And I said Good Evening. There was not the faintest echo, and nobody to listen. So I went inside and played the noblest single theme George Frederic Handel ever composed, the opening of the overture to the *Water Music*. And when that was over, I picked up the newspaper to catch up with the world – with America, that is.

I had made a point – after we got off the plane

from New York and into the clean cold air, as intox-icating as an oxygen mask – of not reading the *New York Times* or the *Wall Street Journal*, or any other paper printed for the enlightenment or discourage-ment of the city folk, or of anyone beyond rural Vermont. There was, delivered by a well-wrapped-up elf every morning, the *local* paper. And there was news enough of America to chew on.

As: the ninety-sixth annual meeting of the local Vermont Audubon Christmas Bird Count was this year about to field ten teams over a designated circle (with a diameter of fifteen miles). Last year they'd spotted fifty-four species, including lots of northern shrikes, bohemian waxwings, pine grosbeaks, the pine siskin, *and* a peregrine falcon. At the end of this year's outing there was to be a 'count-down pot luck supper'.

Hello! Here was a state – a Vermont – record. Muzzle loaders took 661 bucks, in addition to 1,438 antlerless deer by muzzle loaders with special permits. The 1995 bow-and-arrow kill was just over 5,000 deer. And all in all, it says here, 'The total number of whitetails taken in Vermont during the 1995 season, which runs from the end of October into December, should exceed 18,000, which is a state record.' There is no sound, no whimper, in the paper or in life from animal lovers. On the contrary, the environmentalists even breathe relief. Vermont is so heavily overrun with deer that unless so many thou-sands are shot, the herds suffer a lingering death from starvation.

The other record is the number of teams of high school children who collected food and woolies and went out and gave them to the visibly homeless. The very thought of homelessness in Vermont calls up a picture of the original iceman, and I move on.

Day after Christmas, we visited an old couple, very old friends, who have moved into an old folks' home – complete with movie theatre, infirmary, gymnasium, library, sauna, knitting room, dining room (rather lush and much varied menu), central air conditioning all round the year. Day after, we took the plane and zoomed back to what they strangely call civilization – civilization and the *New York Times* – and the hourly news on the telly. I'd also made a point of not watching TV news either. All we saw on the screen was a rented movie called *While You Were Sleeping*. Throughout the movie, the whole family slept.

So, it will take time to catch up with the ordeal of unemployed federal workers in the government shutdown. (In Washington, several thousand of them staged a new kind of protest – a work-in.) The crime news. Good news for once there. A lawyer working for the state of Texas was troubled to discover offhand corruption in a department of the government. He reported it to higher-ups. Nothing happened. He tried again. Nothing. He persisted. He was fired. He lost his pay, he lost his home – for he decided to sue the state for wrongful dismissal. It took time and it cost loads of money. At the end of two years, he was living in a trailer – a caravan, *n'est-ce pas*? Just recently, his case came to trial. The judge awarded him – and an Appeals Court upheld – the sum of, wait for it! Twenty-one million dollars. He is moving out of his caravan.

Bosnia? Well, so far there's nothing but good news there too, except for the soldiers who woke up under floods. Best, most memorable item anyway, was a twenty-second bite on the evening news. A reporter with mike aloft stopped a black soldier at a coffee stall. The soldier was a benevolent character with a chuckling expression and gold-rimmed spectacles. The reporter wanted to know what the soldier thought his mission was. The gold rims turned to the little roadside counter. He said, 'Cheeseburger and a Coke to go.' He chuckled again. 'Mah mission? Why, man, Ah'm gonna save the free world and everybody else.'

POCKET PENGUINS

POCKET PENGUINS